# YELLOW ARROW

Vol. V, No. 2
Spring 2020
*Home*

ISSN 2688-3015 (print)
ISSN 2688-3023 (online)
ISBN 9781735023007 (paperback)

# Yellow Arrow Journal

Nonfiction and poetry by writers that identify as women

Vol. V, No. 2
Spring 2020
*Home*

## Editor-in-Chief
Kapua Iao

## Poetry Editor
Ann Quinn

## Editorial Associates
Bailey Drumm, Kierstin Kessler, Alexa Laharty, Rebecca Massey, and Siobhan McKenna

## Contributors
Paula Bonnell, Andrée Rose Catalfamo, Lindsey Clark, Catherine A. Coundjeris, Diane Vogel Ferri, Cynthia Gallaher, Kashaf Ghumman, Tara Flaherty Guy, Jo Ann Hoffman, Ann Howells, Stephanie Kadel Taras, Roberta S. Kuriloff, J.L. Lapinel, Robinwyn Lewis, Carolyn Martin, Crystal Leigh Melbourne, Courtney Essary Messenbaugh, Sara Palmer, Kara Panowitz, Hannah Rousselot, Nichola Ruddell, Sarah Smith, Amy Soricelli, Elizabeth Spencer Spragins, and Yvonne

## Cover Art
Ann Marie Sekeres

YELLOW ARROW
PUBLISHING

PO Box 12119, Baltimore, MD 21281
info@yellowarrowpublishing.com

*We prioritize the unique voice and
style of each of our authors.*

*Every writer has a story to tell and
every story is worth telling.*

**Yellow Arrow Publishing**

**Clackamas, Oregon**

# *Mandate*
## Carolyn Martin

To those of you who will not die today:
walk through your home and bless the open doors,
the table set, the breadth of sun lounging
on the Persian rug. Catalog the small
contentments you have earned: eager words vying
for a poem, work you'll never have to do
again, backyard squirrels that entertain.
Praise every squill, crocus, and bleeding heart
that dares subvert this winter's calendar.
Invite young mysteries in and seat them
between answers you have no questions for
and ponderables still unclassified.
It goes with saying, listen attentively.
Then tomorrow, if it arrives, repeat.

*It is beautiful to do nothing and rest afterwards.*
*~adopted from a Spanish proverb*

# Table of Contents

*Mandate*     i
Carolyn Martin

Introduction     1
Gwen Van Velsor

Book Review     7
*Landing on Your Feet and Putting Down Roots:*
*21 Rituals to Transform Your Life and Interior Space*
*by Sherry Burton Ways*
Kara Panowitz

*Our Hearth*     11
Courtney Essary Messenbaugh

*Journeys*     13
Elizabeth Spencer Spragins

*Unearthing Home*     15
Roberta S. Kuriloff

*Castaway*     23
Paula Bonnell

*Water Nymph*     25
Crystal Leigh Melbourne

*Deconstructing Dallas*     27
Ann Howells

*Why I Love My Old Room at the Abbey*     29
Jo Ann Hoffman

*Muddy in Morocco*     31
Lindsey Clark

| | |
|---|---|
| *Row Home*<br>Sara Palmer | 37 |
| *BEHIND CLOSED DOORS: The Lena O. Smith House*<br>Yvonne | 39 |
| *Both Sides of Burnside Avenue*<br>Amy Soricelli | 41 |
| *Hickory*<br>Sarah Smith | 43 |
| *Notes to My Predecessor*<br>Stephanie Kadel Taras | 45 |
| *The Art Studio*<br>Diane Vogel Ferri | 47 |
| *The Mehndi on My Feet*<br>Kashaf Ghumman | 55 |
| *displaced*<br>Hannah Rousselot | 57 |
| *Hiraeth*<br>Tara Flaherty Guy | 59 |
| *A Recipe for Greek Bread*<br>Catherine A. Coundjeris | 63 |
| *Blackamora*<br>J.L. Lapinel | 65 |
| *After Georgia O'Keeffe's* Spring 1923/24<br>Cynthia Gallaher | 67 |
| *Blooms*<br>Andrée Rose Catalfamo | 69 |

*Uninvited* 75
Robinwyn Lewis

*Movement in the Cinnabar Valley* 77
Nichola Ruddell

*On the Cover: Couch* 79
Ann Marie Sekeres

*Contributors* 81

Baltimore, Maryland

# *Dear Readers,*

When we selected the theme for this issue, we certainly had no idea how relevant it would be in these days and times. After opening Yellow Arrow House in January 2020, the **HOME** theme for this journal felt like a cozy way to embrace the new shape our organization had taken. We envisioned the House as a place of refuge for writers, where they could gather in community over a shared passion for the written word.

I write to you now, in the middle of spring, and at the height of a crisis. Yellow Arrow House is closed at the moment. May this issue serve as an example of the collective wisdom that is generated when a group of women come together over a common goal. In this case, to create a collection of work that represents all manners of interpreting a sense of home, something we are experiencing, perhaps, in a new way.

To me, home is the place where my soul resides. My spiritual home is in the rooms of a 12-step program. Although I can't physically take part in that particular circle of healing, my spirit continues to reside in the principles of the program. I share this because I hope you have access at this time to your spiritual home, whether it be in memory, in body and blood, with your ancestors, or among loved ones. I hope you are able to ground yourself in the knowing that home is right where you are.

It is our mission at Yellow Arrow to always bring hope and positivity to our publications and to our work. And now, more than ever, we offer this issue to you as a font of goodwill during a time when great healing must be our task.

Although it has been our tradition to produce hand-bound, limited edition copies of the journal, we are unable to gather over needles and thread to sew this time. The hand-bound versions are our way of keeping this work as personal as possible, and we hope that you'll keep in mind the humanness behind the writing here.

While reading this issue, you will notice a bold location at the beginning of each piece (in the top right corner) and an italicized phrase at its end (bottom center). We've asked each author to give us some insight on where they are physically and a mantra or piece of advice that's getting them through this moment. As you hold this book in your hands, think of the women who wrote these words, of all the people who will read the same words, and know that you are not alone.

We don't yet know when our writing home will reopen but it has certainly continued to serve as a refuge for me, since it is the only other place I can safely go. Each morning, my daughter and I pack a bag of snacks and toys and head over to Yellow Arrow House to clean and paint, to dream, and to nest. We look forward to welcoming your creative energy into our home once again.

*Sincerely,*

*Gwen*

Gwen Van Velsor
Founder & President, Yellow Arrow Publishing

*"Pray without ceasing."*
*~1 Thessalonians 5:17*

# HOME

## Book Review
*Landing on Your Feet and Putting Down Roots: 21 Rituals to Transform Your Life and Interior Space*
by Sherry Burton Ways
Reviewed by Kara Panowitz

 When my friend, Holly, read the opening to Yellow Arrow Publishing's first Reading Club book selection, *Landing on Your Feet and Putting Down Roots: 21 Rituals to Transform Your Life and Interior Space*,[1] she started crying. "This is me," she said. "I could have written this." The book opens with author Sherry Burton Ways sharing her personal experience with a relationship ending in divorce. This sets the stage for the book itself: how to transform your physical space, and yourself, after major life transitions. Burton Ways' honesty and openness create a space of trust and relatability. Her recognition that it can feel daunting or too expensive to make transformations during significant life changes brings comfort, and her story demonstrates that no space is too small to create a refuge or a home. In her own words, Burton Ways' goal for writing this book is to show readers "how their interior design can assist them with additional support" (pg. 4).

 Burton Ways' explanation that "interior design is not decorating" (5) is a theme that carries throughout the rituals she presents. The biggest lesson I took away was that home is not just a physical space and group of objects, but the rituals and aspects of your life you bring to it and how they all connect together. The 21 rituals presented include some that might be expected, like rearranging furniture, selecting interior colors, and creating vision boards. Others I found less expected, such as the ritual of bathing and loving yourself through environment and crystal energy.

---

[1] Published by FriesenPress in 2017, 112 pages; hardcover (978-1-5255-0556-0), paperback (978-1-5255-0557-7), or e-book (978-1-5255-0558-4). For more about Burton Ways, visit sherryburtonways.com.

Finally, there were rituals completely new to me, like Wabi-sabi.[2]

One of the most useful and most accessible things about the book is that it presents actions you can take immediately or in the near future, which you can continue daily or just once in a while. You make it work for you. Burton Ways' 21 rituals also come with tips and ideas, taking the abstract to the specific. There is something for everyone in this book and it may make you look at something you hadn't really considered, or perhaps thought wasn't for you, in a new way.

The rituals explored in *Landing on Your Feet and Putting Down Roots* also give new ideas for, and new meaning to, rituals you may already perform. The ritual of music and dance spoke to me the most. *Why don't I listen to music and dance more*? I love both, and I can influence the mood and energy in my home through what I choose to listen to, and how I groove to it. Burton Ways' descriptions made me think of music and dance affecting and permeating my space, spreading through the air and seeping into the walls (I danced that night!). She addresses the physical space by suggesting that readers create open space for dance and carry music into that physical space by displaying artwork that depicts music or even instruments.

Additionally, I enjoy the ritual of cooking but don't always want to do it or give much thought to the process. When I read about it in the book, it brought new mindfulness and value to meal preparation and my place in it. Burton Ways writes,

> "Cooking is an interior abundance ritual that can relieve stress and give your life a sense of purpose during major life transitions. Meal preparation allows you to have control over your life and express yourself . . . [and] is an anti-stress exercise because the process of cooking activates the senses that have been numbed" (45).

I thought about cooking in a new way, in terms of how it influences

---

[2] Wabi-sabi is a Japanese aesthetics, a world view centered on the acceptance of transience and imperfection.

and spreads throughout my space, similar to music.

Burton Ways includes personal experiences by other women, intended for readers "to see [themselves] in this process" (4). These candid and insightful stories illuminate how rituals can be used in transitions, including divorce, death, a new career, and even constant change due to housing insecurity. It reaffirms that you can choose and adjust your rituals for any situation, and that something as small as a handheld rock can bring comfort and consistency during transitions. Burton Ways also shares examples from clients she has worked with that demonstrate the implementation of her rituals in an array of spaces. The stories are inspirational and a highlight of the book.

As I read *Landing on Your Feet and Putting Down Roots*, I felt like Burton Ways was a friend, mentor, and coach, and that we were blessed to have a visit from her for Yellow Arrow's Reading Club. This author has many talents and a diverse array of expertise: she is an award winning author, trainer, and speaker, and holds several certifications such as Certified Design Psychology Coach, Certified Graceful Lifestyles Consultant, and Certified Interior Environment Coach. Her passion for her work is evident in the guidance she shares on her pages.

This was a perfect book for Yellow Arrow's first Reading Club session because Yellow Arrow House in Baltimore, Maryland had just opened, and one of the primary missions of Yellow Arrow is to create a safe, welcoming refuge that feels like home, within the House and within workshops and events. The timing was also serendipitous for me because I was living alone in a new apartment and was ready to embrace transition. I immediately made changes to my space and life after reading the book and continue to revisit her words for reminders and ideas on how to implement her 21 rituals.

Finally, as I wrote this review, the COVID-19 pandemic forced everyone to spend a lot more time at home, and I began to use the rituals to ease anxiety and keep creativity flowing. That's one of the greatest gifts of Sherry Burton Ways' book. You can always revisit it to change your space and your life in small or big ways. Like life, changes are not always permanent. No matter what your reason for transforming your space and life, *Landing on Your Feet and Putting Down Roots* will speak to you and encourage you to find rituals to comfort and support yourself during times of transition.

*Give what you can, take what you need.*

Lafayette, Colorado

# *Our Hearth*
## Courtney Essary Messenbaugh

The moon must get tired from
Doing all that it has to do. Pushing and

Pulling the tides. Waxing and waning
In size. Engorging itself to inspire

Howling monsters, thick with legend, while
Awaiting its next set of footprints. And yet,

It still finds the energy to stay in the sky
Long after its duties in darkness are done,

Looking like a filmy piece of tracing
Paper during the light. Perhaps to remind us

That we too toil and endure and persist with
The power to send a highway of sparks

Through the blackness here on Earth.

*Be patient with and kind to yourself and others.*

Fredericksburg, Virginia

## *Journeys*
### Elizabeth Spencer Spragins

**From Afar**
the moon rests her oars
and rolls her weary shoulders
a breath before dawn
when I lose my way in dreams
wrens and robins sing me home
                ~Annapolis, Maryland

**Back to Earth**
an autumn rain hums
as she wanders realms of roots—
seeds tucked in cradles
drink the wine of warmer days
and remember faded blooms
                ~Charleston, South Carolina

**Hiraeth\***
a restless spring moon
combs the beaches at low tide—
so many journeys
leave no footprints on the path
but my longing leads me home
                ~Beaufort, North Carolina

\*A Welsh word meaning an intense longing for home.

*When we get to the other side.*

## *Unearthing Home*
### Roberta S. Kuriloff

> "Our soul is an abode. And by remembering 'houses' and 'rooms,' we learn to 'abide' within ourselves."
> From Gaston Bachelard's *The Poetics of Space*

*What was I thinking*? I'm 39, lived my life mainly in cities, and now I'm moving to the woods of Maine. Alone. On this blustery March day, I stand at the edge of the land in Maine I purchased with my former partner, a shared plan no longer to be. My hands tingle from the cold as I hold the wood stakes that will mark off exactly where my new house will be. Excited. Anxious. My chest tightens as ripples of fear move through me.

The foundation of my first home with my parents collapsed before I barely lived there, before I barely understood the meaning of home. *Is that going to happen again*? When I was six years old, I lived in an apartment in New York with my parents and two-year-old brother. I had a family. I felt safe and secure. I had no worries. I learned only too well at that tender age that life can collapse as quickly as a child's smile can morph into tears.

I shudder with the memory of those tears. I see myself in my parents' bedroom, standing on my tiptoes. At the time, I could barely see my mother in bed under a white canopy hanging down from the bedposts. I felt like a spy. My eyes made out only her form, but I knew she could see me. I asked, "Daddy, can I go on the bed with Mommy?" My mother said yes and Dad lifted me up. I cuddled into her right arm. Smelled her warmth. The scent of lilac wafted over me. I wanted to stay there, tight against her body forever. My father's face was haggard, his eyes sad. A few days later the bed was empty. When I asked my father where she was, he told me she was in the hospital. I never saw her again.

I shake as I dig the holes for the wood stakes to set the lines of my house foundation. Perhaps it is only restlessness, but I suspect it is more. The surrounding tall trees, open fields, and fresh air remind me of my aunt and uncle's farm in New Jersey—another home destroyed by the emotional tornado of death.

At their farm, I played in the large hay mill. I learned from my uncle how to corral the cows and milk them, and to feed the chickens. I helped my aunt care for my brother and cook meals. My father worked in the city as a cab driver and came "home" to the farm on weekends. I missed him, but I relished the farm and felt as if I were living in the Bronx Zoo. Dad and my uncle made me a swing hung from a tall tree that stood near the river.

A year later my aunt's body filled with cancer, like my mother's. Almost as quickly as we arrived, my idyllic year was over. Then a few months later, my father moved me and my brother to the Israel Orphan Asylum, an orphanage in Queens, New York.

Permanence. My intellectual side knows there is no such thing, but the child I once was continues to search for that "forever-after" place, a home that cannot be lost or taken away. *Do I define home for myself or is it defined for me by childhood circumstances over which I have no control*? Circumstances that also change the meaning of family. *Does my need for a meaningful home control my life choices*? These questions have challenged me in therapy—a healthy challenge I've accepted.

Before moving to Maine, I had taken a building workshop to bolster my belief in my strength and endurance. It helped me appreciate how much I mastered in the orphanage to toughen up and survive, even when that toughness was a veiled disguise. It's not easy for this lawyer's fingers and shoulders to change from typing to banging nails into a roof! Yet, here I am—ex-secretary, lawyer, feminist, and political activist, giving up a meaningful life in New Haven and getting ready to build my own home, trying to rediscover, maybe redefine myself again.

I walk around the smooth ground surrounding my new foundation. The beginning of a new security blanket. Like the deep-rooted oak, maple, and pine trees encircling the foundation on the north and west sides of my potential house to protect it from winter winds and storms, I am establishing new roots, hopefully to be as deep-seated and secure as these trees. I walk over to an old tree stump and note its rings of aged growth. I remind myself that not all trees weather the storm.

Memories surge of other deep-rooted trees surrounding my first day in the orphanage, when my father walked my brother, now age four, and me, now age seven, through a tall, black wrought iron gate leaving us with a tall and bent smoky-haired woman. She took us to two different buildings, separated by an expanse of trees and hedges and cement. We only got together when my father visited with us on most weekends.

*****

I'm currently living in a rented mobile home three miles from my land while I build my dream. I hired two women—Sue and Niki—to help me, one of whom taught the housebuilding workshop I took. Both have strong personalities, like me. I'm usually in control of my work circumstances. Here, I'm out of my element. But we work well together. I quickly discover the workshop didn't teach me as much as I thought. Even the building information in the books I read do not stick in my brain when it comes to the actual work. One day, as we break for lunch, sitting on the grass eating our sandwiches, Sue smiles and says, "Don't be so hard on yourself. It will get easier." I laugh and say, "I hope so. I don't think I'm made for this work, but it's special being part of the intricate building of my house. I'm in awe."

After finishing the floor of the house, we put up the wall studs, the anchors of the house, to hold it tall and strong against the Maine winds, just as the winds of circumstance have pushed me to where I now stand.

How often in the heat of emotion, or when confronted with unwanted surprises, have I contemplated whether I'm surviving or thriving, a mantra I have tried to recapture when I'm falling apart. How hard it is during such times to find internal space to reflect! I am not Superwoman. I am a woman seeking the meaning of the human experience—an ongoing challenge, especially as I struggle to find my inner housebuilder.

*****

I've been in Maine now for two months. The early June weather is mostly mellow with soft breezes. My clothes and body are sprayed with protection from the blackflies. A lot of people swear by Avon's Skin So Soft bath oil as a cure to keep the blackflies away. Since it is difficult nailing while wearing my hat and insect netting, I start using the bath oil even though it feels slippery and I smell like a mix of potent perfumes from the makeup counter in Macy's.

My body is stronger but aches like when I once fell off my bike as a child, accelerating downhill. I've now made a new friend, a chiropractor, to help with the pain in my shoulders and back. Law books are easier to carry than studs and beams.

As we finish the second floor of my unfinished house, I challenge my unfinished self. I stretch skyward with a smile, hands in the air, looking forward to the open world around me, and think of the words from Helen Reddy's song "I Am Woman":

> I am strong
> I am invincible
> I am woman

My strength is lifted by my memories. I accept I cannot be adept at everything I do, even though the little girl in me would like to be—to have total control, to never be hurt or disappointed, to know it all. For now, I'm okay being a kid playing with blocks, carrying joists, dropping the joists, and hammering my fingers instead of nails. This kid is building a house!

*****

A few more months pass and the outside of the house is almost finished, as well as the inside insulation and sheetrock, the latter of which a specialist is handling. Walls and space seem to determine my interior needs. I proactively make my own choices: light–dark, privacy, room size. A new sense of the word home. *Am I yet my own person, undefined by the outside world*? I doubt so. But each step is forward-moving.

I name my property Crumblesweat. People often ask me what the name means. I joke that "I'm crumbling under the sweat of designing and building my home." A little true. But really, the name came to me in a dream months before, when my mind was in the processing stage. The dream confirmed my daunting choice to relocate.

*****

After moving in, I discover that the two windows in the living room become mirrors at night when the outside lights are on, and I dance and exercise as if I'm in a dance studio, with my only audience the tall pine and oak trees. No shades or blinds. Windows everywhere. The kitchen has two windows of its own, one on the north and the other on the east. The dining room also faces east with two tall windows. When I eventually sit at my dining room table, I will look through the sliding glass door on the south and the morning sun through the east windows.

Downstairs there is a bathroom off the bedroom, and even though I have lived in apartments and houses with a private bathroom, a sadness still strikes me, thinking of the shared bathrooms and open showers in the orphanage. I won't forget, I am a lucky kid!

When I stand on the deck and look out at the openness around me, part of me dreams of a house made fully of glass. Silly idea! I thought I lost the feeling of being a stranger in a strange land, closed in, but I discovered it never goes away, just buried in some hidden cells of my body.

Every time I moved, I felt like an outsider. Now I'm framing a new life—not the frame of the fields past the wrought iron gate of the orphanage, nor the frame of the cow pasture on my aunt's farm, nor the streets and small trees outside the Brooklyn apartment in which we lived with Dad when we left the orphanage. Let alone my first apartment in New York City and my apartment in Boston during law school. I temporarily lost the strangeness when living with my partner in New Haven, in a cute small house with a white picket fence. Now that is a melancholy memory, albeit at least a meaningful friendship.

I ponder how my life would be if I had a mother, especially during my teen years. In a recent therapy session, a burst of soul-stirring pain shot through me as I encountered, head on, the little girl in me. Wrenched from her mother, then her father. Put in a strange place. Feeling like a hostage. I couldn't leave. No parents to protect me. Separated from my brother. Controlled by adults I didn't know. I recollect my brother's frightened face, but not mine.

*****

It is an early crisp fall day, the first rays of dawn lighting the sky, and I'm finally living in my new home with my three cats and one dog, Maya. I take Maya for a walk up our private dirt road, to the more traveled dirt road with only two houses on it. My house is hidden in the woods by fields. My only neighbor is at the head, where the private road meets the traveled one.

I sit alone in my work clothes at the kitchen table sipping tea, the rough skin on my hands circling the hot cup. There is still much work to complete in my corner of heaven. The subfloor is plywood, needing to be covered with flooring. The walls require painting. The windows and doors lack trim. The stark ceiling reveals insulation wrapped in plastic, like an arid desert, eventually to be finished in pine tongue and groove. The walkway upstairs, along the brick chimney, needs a bannister, as do the steps. The kitchen cabinets need doors. The list goes on. Two friends drop by with loads of plants for me to adopt, adding color and warmth.

On a hazy cool day, a little later, the earthy scent of smoke from other woodstoves wafts through the woods, reminding me of browning marshmallows by a fire. Friends visit to help stack my woodpile. We cover the pile with large blue tarps to protect it from rain and snow, pinning the ends down like a tent into the ground. I'm getting ready for my first Maine winter in my new home. At night, I bring in a handful of wood to practice how best to utilize my woodstove, having learned from friends. Sometimes I screw up. One night I rush to the screen door holding a burning piece of wood with my stove glove and throw it outside on a pile of dirt. The house is smoky and the cats hide.

I sit on a small rug in the living room and unpack family and vacation albums, wistfully recapturing my memories. Dad loved to take pictures; black and white ones from before my mother's death, some from the orphanage, others of my high school years, and our family trips after reliving together. I laugh at how, as a teenager, I sloppily reinforced them in albums with scotch tape and staples. I find forgotten pictures of friends and visits with my cousins, aunts, and uncles. So little time spent with them during my childhood, more so during my teenage years.

A morning after a leisurely walk with Maya, I unpack my diaries and journals. My first diary—a three by three inch pink diary, now with a broken lock and aged white paper—was given to me by a cousin as a gift at age 12 when my brother and I left the orphanage. I laugh at my penciled handwriting and the silly things I wrote. Then I read my confusion, the bewildered emotions of my new life outside the orphanage, missing childhood friends. I close the diary; I'm not ready to relive them yet.

Instead, I put some small framed pictures on the chimney mantles with some knickknacks, including the bones of a deer head and chin Maya found when we early on visited the property. I transported from New Haven an odd-looking table found at a yard sale that was once a wooden cable spool and later served as a coffee table. Now it sits covered with newspapers and folders in front of my red and black checkered two-seated couch.

The house is becoming a home, my home, even though unfinished. In several years it will be finished, filled with warmth, new love shared, and colorful gardens.

Now, I sit alone at my table eating eggs and toast and look out the sliding glass door to the open space and woods. I smile with surprise as I see a moose slowly walking across the property, his long legs stepping over a huge rock as if it is a pebble. *Am I surviving or thriving?* Yes. With all the changes I've gone through, *I am thriving. I will thrive.* I am home.

"Life will always be sorrowful. We can't change it, but we can change our attitude toward it." ~Joseph Campbell

## *Castaway*
### Paula Bonnell

The island is not a desert, and Drusilla,
the good hen who had nested in the lifeboat I took,
pecks in the clearing and shares my crumbs.
Yesterday she laid her first egg.
The sun is insistent, golden, singular;
the juice of these berries I have found
stains well enough to serve as ink.
The currents are uncertain, our latitude
and longitude—unknown. I would ask
for a cat, but for Drusilla and the lack of
an address to which to forward it.
Books are what I chiefly need.
If I could make soap, glass—yet
I have a toolbox, driftwood has given me
enough to build a hut on a platform.
I have a rope hammock and fish,
the odd fruits of the assorted trees.
The hardtack is nearly gone. Yes,
I wish for yeast and grain and,
above all, for stories, the considered
music of words, for laughter, but the cooler season
has begun, and I have my work,
my sturdy hat, and the silver
setting of the sun.

*Attention and balance are the two big goals of social life and solving problems.*

Mainz, Rheinland-Pfalz, Germany

## *Water Nymph*
### Crystal Leigh Melbourne

The city has a way of luring me into its heaviness
disguised as hectic karaoke nights at Baby Grand's
where drinking's religion and I hold God in my hands
like a moth dizzying itself around a golden flame,
I feel everything to the core yet none of it makes sense,
it doesn't have to. Truth is when it's time to go home I lie
jabbering on about having had the most wondrous time
and how I wish I could stay for everything here's divine,
truth is I get exhausted easily from these fluorescent lights
so off I am barefoot on shimmering asphalt, seven miles
of passing through flickering films, on and off, it seems,
in attempts to wrap me back around in its metallic wires
but I've got the ocean in me longing for Galene's quiet.
The wisest say only turbulent spirits are drawn to the sea,
that only stormy hearts simmer down under the salt of it—
so let it be.
    As I'm drenched in sweet cadence, bathing in waveforms,
my silvery soul rejoices drifting further from the shore,
and a sudden feeling of comfort washes over me.
I'm finally Home.

*This is a time to decompress, to slow down.*
*Now we can finally learn to breathe at our own pace.*

## *Deconstructing Dallas*
### Ann Howells

The city unfolds like an origami crane.
Night shivers with recognition,
and I revel in each small wonder:
orange barrels overseeing construction
along Northwest Highway;
blinking traffic lights at Royal Lane
moving traffic car by car—
east/west, north/south.
I slow for the bump where Forest
crosses Midway, pass the dry cleaner,
high school playing field, and shop
where I bought my tulip lamp.
Three miles of smooth resurfaced road
tempt my foot to press harder.
Blue lights of Arapaho Bridge appear,
iron arches against cobalt sky,
picturesque local rival to the Eiffel Tower.
Roadways remain damp
with small puddles from an earlier rain,
and the moon appears muzzy
viewed through a fragile atmosphere
that still cups me in its trembling hand.

*Think carefully before acting on any information you receive.*

Cary, North Carolina

## *Why I Love My Old Room at the Abbey*\*
### Jo Ann Hoffman

It isn't large, but large enough.
You can't stand in the center, for instance,
and touch opposing walls.
Let's say it's eight by ten:
one window, small; one blanket, thin.
The floor is bare, the water, cold.
A narrow bed, a desk, a chair.
The lamps are bright and cozy, by the way,
and the standing box for heat and air
blasts its little heart out.
This night—or surely morning now—
I turn the heater off despite the January cold,
wanting respite from the great white noise
of constant circulating fan.
The silence wraps around me
like a deep blue velvet arm.
I listen to its nothingness.

And then—sweet sound—the abbey bells
arise upon the silence, round and pure,
threading pines and trailing fields across the winter dark,
gathering the monks to watch the night.
My dreamy smile spreads slowly—then it soars
beyond the ceiling, through the roof, into the stars.
White fingers of cold curl beneath the doorframe.
I hug my hapless pillow
and find my meager blanket
very warm.

\* The Trappist monks of Mepkin Abbey replaced the old guesthouse in 2013.

*Write one image as a private primer for personal creativity
throughout the day.*

## *Muddy in Morocco*
Lindsey Clark

The spring rains of northern Morocco mist the land like a gauzy veil, as if to remind an interloper such as me of the exhilarating, unnerving, and unknowability of this land and its people. Saharan desert and parched Kasbahs were my major preconceptions of North Africa but are actually hallmarks of the southern Maghreb. In the more temperate north, the buildup to summer is overwhelmingly damp. Unlike the torrential downpours of a jungle, the mild intensity and duration of the spring rains should not cause much inconvenience. Yet when the rains showered the foothills of the Rif Mountains just a month after I had arrived in the tiny, off-grid subsistence-farming village called Zawiet Sidi Chaaib, they surprised me like a slap in the face—another reminder of the deep mysteriousness and unpredictability of the place I was trying to call home.

My house sat, tucked amid a grove of olive trees, itself nestled in the patchwork quilt of wheat fields that blanketed occasional respites of flat ground, surrounded by steep slopes of sheep pasture and vegetable terracing. Locals welcomed the rains as lifeblood. But as regular showers quenched the thirst of the countryside of the Taza region that April, the clay content of the southern edge of the Rif mountain range emerged to pose yet another unexpected challenge in my new surroundings.

The mud! The mud became the medium of my days and my imprisoner. It was impossible to leave my house (incidentally, made of mud) for anything without engaging in an unintended mud-wrestling practice: me versus the slickened clay. With each step, I gambled whether the mud would stick (creating false and dangerously uneven three-inch platform shoes) or slide (landing me on my ass with an immediate scan of the horizon to check for laughing witnesses). Even under a teasing sun, the mud would barely begin to solidify before a fresh rain restored it to the consistency of slimy old oatmeal.

One day that spring, I returned to the village from Taza with a week's worth of books, mail, food, and other sundries jammed tightly into my camping backpack and overflowing into souq bags slung over each shoulder. The nearest paved road was seven kilometers from my house, and no public transport served that final, mud-tortured stretch to the hamlet I called home. When a shared taxi dropped me at the turnoff and then lurched eagerly westward toward Fes, I turned to face my adversary. The way north was not so much a road as a formidable expanse of gush, rough with the water-filled craters of donkey hoofprints. I was top-heavy with supplies. This would not be pretty. The only positive omen I had going for me was a break in the rain and the sun shining encouragingly.

As I began the slow slog up the trail, every second or third step had my weighted foot either sinking a couple of inches into the goo or immediately shooting out from under me, which resulted in a desperate pinwheeling of my arms in an attempt to regain my balance. Before long, my arms and back were fighting the weight of my bags with a dull, irritating ache. The constant discomfort was punctuated by the sudden, dangerous pulling of my muscles when I made sudden movements to keep my balance.

In order to distract myself from my painful and tedious forward progress, I began to mentally catalog the many ways this mud trail was a metaphor for the intimidating and sometimes slippery terrain of my experience living and working in rural northern Morocco. When I removed my shoes and socks to wade across a stretch of underwater road, two farmers crossing an adjacent field stopped to watch me with obvious amusement and confirmed my feeling that inadvertently entertaining the local population was perhaps my most important role here. Scrambling up a ridge of olive trees adjacent to one muddy patch (so deep-looking I was certain it would swallow me whole if I attempted to cross) reminded me of my attempts to skirt the quagmire of village

politics that threatened to sink every project I undertook.
   On I trod, one timid and unsteady foot in front of the other, kilometer by kilometer. Every so often, I forced myself to look up and appreciate the rolling hills around me: rich earthy browns, greens, and yellows topped by bright blue as a backdrop to wispy clouds. In the setting sun, I knew this scenery would turn pastel like something from an illustrated book of fairytales. I neared a meditative state, where I ceased to believe it could really be me—an unremarkable person from an unremarkable suburb of an unremarkable state in the American Midwest—who had been walking for what felt like years in this remote corner of North Africa for some reason I probably once knew but could no longer remember. Everything I carried, its weight locking my muscles into a stubborn resistance, seemed unnecessary and useless to my life or anyone else's. I kept walking, disassociated but at peace, without even really knowing why. I was just a person on this planet, like every other person on this planet. And in that I found the lightness needed to keep moving forward through that mud.
   At the edge of the village stood a building housing two competing hanoots (convenience stores), owned and run by brothers. This mutually unbeneficial competition was something I never understood. One of the brothers, though nearly deaf, warmly shook my hand and engaged me in jovial conversation each time I passed his store.
   "Salaam, Layla," he smiled, greeting me with the Arabic name I had agreed to adopt rather than forcing my Moroccan friends and neighbors to pronounce the jumble of consonants in my actual name.
   "Salaam," I replied.
   "Shnoo?" he asked. *What*?
   "SALAAM!" screamed his brother, directly into his ear. The deaf hanoot man smiled benignly at both of us, then rattled off a quick sentence. I had been studying Derija, the Moroccan dialect of Arabic, for three months, but I understood not a single word of

what he said to me.

"Shnoo?" I asked. His brother repeated the sentence, screaming toward me, and the deaf hanoot owner and I both looked at him in alarm. I still had no idea what was happening. Finally, the deaf hanoot man spread his arms in a grand gesture encompassing the entire path.

"Gheis!" he exclaimed. *Mud!*

"Wa, gheis bizef!" I yelled back at him. *Yes, a lot of mud!*

He gave a belly laugh before literally shoving me back into motion toward my house. My near-delirium made me see magic in this moment: trodding through the mud mired in great misunderstanding, but an even greater interpersonal warmth that fueled and propelled me onward.

As I approached the slipperiest part of the steepest hill I had to climb, a neighbor woman riding a horse through the muck caught up with me from behind and offered me a ride. After nearly five miles on the mud road, I was tired enough to accept gratefully, despite what I already knew it would cost me: the effort of diplomatically deflecting her invitation to marry me off to one of her sons. The kindness of others was the only reason I was surviving as a foreigner here, but I had learned kindness can be a form of currency, and I could never be sure what might be expected as repayment. The villagers expressed vehement and constant opinions about me, my life choices, and my future. At 25 years old, my spinsterhood loomed imminently. My insistence on living alone and traveling to and from Taza on my own appalled and alarmed all of my friends and neighbors (they were sure there were murderers in the next town over; the people in that town thought the same of the people in my village). That my independent streak might make me unfit to be a good Muslim wife in rural Morocco seemed not to have occurred to anyone but me. During the past month, I had spent hours upon hours thinking about the absurd dissonance between who I thought I was and who my neighbors thought I should be. I had been driving myself crazy with philosophical questions of identity, judgment, and culture. But now, like the ground giving way to mud under the inevitability of these rains, I felt too mushy to care much anymore.

With thanks, but with my single status intact, I slid down from the equine transport when we reached the final footpath to my house. The weight of my bags settled again on my back and shoulders. Pausing for a deep breath, I steeled myself for the final 300 yards between me and the mud-free comforts of my little abode. This should have been the best part of the walk—so close, so close—but it was the worst because it was the steepest. Just. Keep. Going. One foot in front of the other. Two steps forward, one slip back. Almost there. I imagined my feet cozy in fresh socks and shoes, the cup of tea I would make and sip as the gathering clouds began to empty themselves onto the fields yet again, and the book I would read as darkness fell, no concern since I would be safe, dry, and—

Then, a very wrong step. My right foot plunged ankle-deep into the mud. I yanked it loose, nearly losing my balance under my top-heavy load. My leg came free but the hiking sandal stayed behind. I sighed, set my souq bags down into the sloppy mess, dropped to my knees, and began to dig for it. *So this is it*, I thought, *I am clawing a hole in this mud and the only thing I get to choose is my reaction*. I tried to calm my mind and focus on the task. I channeled the endurance of the relentless rain that made this mess. As soon as I could get a couple of fingers under one end of the shoe, I pried it up, imagining myself as superhuman. With a juicy **SHLOOK** it was liberated from the slick clay. I started to scrape off enough of the mud to put it back on but realized the pointlessness. Briefly, I considered crawling up the steep incline from there. But the neighbors were surely watching. So I picked up all of my bags and stumbled, half-clod, the best I could the rest of the way to my house.

Panting, I unlocked the garishly blue front door, stepped inside, and dropped my bags. It had been only two days since I left, but

I felt a rush of nostalgic gratitude upon seeing this room as I had left it. The few things I had brought from the States were scattered among an ever-increasing volume of blankets, trinkets, and pillows I had collected from Moroccan souqs. My life before was blending into my life now.

    As I turned to close the door, I noticed the leaves of the olive trees rustling in the breeze portending a rain shower. The sun slanted low and golden through breaks in the clouds. A distant donkey brayed. A closer chicken clucked. The kitten recently given to me by a neighbor to ward off mice tore into the room from the inner courtyard to greet me. All these things, I realized, would simply feel normal now if I had not paused to appreciate them. I shut and locked the blue door behind me, still a stranger in a strange land, brought to my knees by earth and water. Yet deep relief rose up inside me, followed by the realization that for the first time in this foreign place, I had the sense of being home.

*Be kind.*

Baltimore, Maryland

## *Row Home*
### Sara Palmer

Libby perches
on her marble stoop,
sunny haven for gray-haired gossips.
The winter was hard, so cold,
so many days snowed in,
cooped up in the sewing room
or keeping Eddie company,
watching his football.
But now she's out.

She sits with her cronies,
three to the top step
like they always do,
matrons, laid back,
taking a break from
soaps and the laundry.

She feels so alive—suddenly
tuned in to their cackle,
alert to the crackle,
crisp chips crunched
in multiple mouths.
They pass the bag
back and forth, easy
old friends. Old Bay
tickles their tongues
between sips of pop
and stories swapped.

Libby perches
on her marble stoop,
proud of this
monument to her
perfect scrubbing that
hides its years.
You would never know
Libby watched (from this same stoop)
her kids riding trikes,
blaring boom boxes,
driving off in souped-up cars;

that she bounced each grandbaby
right here, on her arthritic knees,
served crab cakes on paper plates
while she and Eddie shot the breeze;
cried, on the day her mother died;
laughed on the day her daughter
came home with a ring on her finger.

Libby turns her head,
looks up to the afternoon sun,
judges the time 'til supper.
Satisfied, she soaks it up,
the hot, hard marble
warming her bottom,
the sudden thrill
of contentment, here
on her marble stoop,
now, in this first flush of spring.

*Go outside, sit quietly with yourself, do something you love,*
*and be kind to others.*

Philadelphia, Pennsylvania

## *BEHIND CLOSED DOORS:*
### *The Lena O. Smith House\**
Yvonne

Daybreak. Recess ends. Dreams thicken to walls,
Shadows harden to wood, the mind stumbles
Before duty's bedside clock screams nonsense
Back into mute corners. Honest pretense,
Hardly masquerade of a girlish soul,
But her workaday twin, begins ritual:
Long midnight braids unraveled, her unbound
Victory flag, then recoiled, pinned, unflown;
Further unsexed in the dark suit, white shirt
And tie of the legal tribe; armed for court,
As if for war with stubborn briefcase clout;
Her weekday pocketbook, an afterthought.

Ever punctual, her home witnessed all. . . .
That last day. . . . How the floor cradled her fall.

*The redoubtable civil rights attorney, Lena O. Smith (1855–1966), lived at 3905 Fifth Avenue South in Minneapolis, Minnesota. Her house was added to the National Register of Historic Places in 1991. The first African American woman to practice law in Minnesota and the first woman president of the Minneapolis chapter of the NAACP, Smith is most famed for her successful outcomes in the Arthur and Edith Lee case, the Curtis Jordan case, and the Nicollet Hotel case. For years she led protests against the public screening of *The Birth of a Nation*.

*The first and last country is home.*

## *Both Sides of Burnside Avenue*
### Amy Soricelli

I'm not from the same Bronx as you are.
Mine was dirt roads before the dirt,
and all the Russian ladies wore dark clothing
to buy pickles.
When I met your Bronx it was angry with knives
holed up in a corner, with no lunch money,
and maybe a bad father.
One side of my Bronx was a Hebrew school where
I buried my soul every other Sunday.
Girls with older brothers whispered marble words
into each other's ears, and I brought home fables
about deserts and heroes with the same names
as my uncles.
Your Bronx woke up early in the lazy morning
kicking beer cans and smoking weed.
There were lots of lost dogs in your Bronx.
They were held tight by chains and roamed
in packs.
I would see the Bronx for the way the bell rang
at the end of the year, and how the Motown
settled with us on the front steps.
My Bronx was special occasion cards with glitter
messaged-roses pasted across the front.
Your Bronx kept the best words in its mouth.

*Try to find a tiny good thing in each and every day.*

Baltimore, Maryland

## *Hickory*
### Sarah Smith

It takes about nine hours to get to Hickory,
a town at the foothills of the North Carolina mountains.
We always arrive at dusk or later.
Headlights reflect against the olive green exterior
as we turn into my grandmother's gravel driveway.

I sleep on the couch in the front room.
The pillow cover is dark with flowers, the fabric scratchy.
Passing traffic wakes me in the morning.
Paperweights in the curio gleam in the daylight—
air bubbles frozen in time.

She and my parents play cribbage.
They count cards and runs.
I listen to the language of a game I do not know how to play,
the stream of numbers entrancing, magical.

I spend a week with her in the summer.
In the afternoon, we nap in her bedroom.
She has me read to her.
It is a hardbound book, dull yellow cover, no jacket.
I do not follow the story.
She drowses.
I skip paragraphs to get to the end of the chapter.
She does not notice.
I slide the book onto the end table and fall asleep.

At the time, it was awkward.
I appreciate it now:
this is how she understands love.

*Be outside as much as possible, especially if the sun is out,
and stay active.*

Ann Arbor, Michigan

## *Notes to My Predecessor*
### Stephanie Kadel Taras

From this front window that is ninety
years here this year
I peer at crows who
decorate branches under
the fierce white wind
and neighbors bundled huddled
in scarf and hood
heading home to trouble and good.

You, scores ago, saw this scene.
And another, years from now, might
watch these crows' daughters
as clouds pass the same
winter branches framed then
in wavy, tired glass.

I know no more of you than she will of me.
Nothing of your work or worth
your desires or talents or gnawing fears of
monthly bills or another mouth to feed.
Did you too sit in this window and chew your lip?
Or smile as two robins dipped
toward the softening earth?

No matter.

We have shared this shelter
from the gloaming, you and I,
warmed against winter,
knowing it will not last.

*Don't squander your solitude.*

Solon, Ohio

## The Art Studio
### Diane Vogel Ferri

She was like the other moms in my little world, who cleaned and cooked and hung clothes on a line in the backyard, who had no other identity than their children. Mom kissed me goodbye in the morning and was sitting on the front porch stoop when I walked home. I would tell her about my day and she listened as though she had nothing else to do. She brushed her hair and put on lipstick, looking perfect, before my dad came home from work each day.

Because she was born during the Great Depression, there had been no money for lessons or college. She learned to play the piano by listening to her sister play and became a church organist and a soloist, but those talents were not what roiled inside of her. Nothing compared to the ardent reinvention I would witness later in my life.

*****

One day, I came home from school to find my mom not on the front porch, but lying on the couch, unmoving, smiling weakly at me. I set about taking care of my younger brother and sister, as the eldest child in the family typically did. Mom was not sick but something was wrong.

Things began to change in our house. Sometimes she went to classes in the evening. The large storage room over the garage emptied out. Baseboard heaters and a skylight were installed. New lighting and wooden shelves appeared, and my mother began her life as an artist. It took boldness and determination for my mother to make such changes in her late 40s.

There's a *Dick Van Dyke Show* episode from the early 1960s in which Laura skims some money off of her weekly house allowance and stashes it in a glove in her drawer. One day Rob finds it and confronts her. Humiliated and angry, she cries in the way only Laura Petrie could cry and tells Rob she was saving it to buy him something special. The episode highlighted how little autonomy women had back then, even with understanding husbands. I can't imagine being beholden to someone else in this way.

I often think about other women I watched on television growing up. On *Bewitched*, Samantha Stevens had to give up her witchcraft, a part of herself, to marry Darren. On *Green Acres*, the theme song includes Oliver singing, "You are my wife!" Lisa's response is a sad, "Goodbye, city life." She loves New York and hates the country, but she is his wife! And of course, there were the *I Love Lucy* reruns where Lucy calls Ricky "Sir" and occasionally gets spanked for spending too much money. He certainly wouldn't consider allowing her to fulfill her dream in show business. Just the title, *Father Knows Best*, says it all. *The Honeymooners* was famous for Ralph threatening to send Alice "to the moon" with a fist if she didn't comply. Worst of all, was Jeannie calling Tony "Master" in *I Dream of Jeannie* and catering to his every whim. There were multiple single father shows, but for most of my impressionable years, not a solitary capable, professional woman.

Several times a year we'd pile into the wood-sided Rambler station wagon and travel for two hours to my grandmother's tiny apartment. She and my cousins lived in a small town on the Ohio River, across from filthy steel mills, where we would breathe dirty air and come in blackened from playing outside. My grandmother raised six children there, and every one of them aspired to be musicians, artists, and writers, as did she.

Widowed in her 50s, with little to her name, my grandmother sat alone in her humble apartment, year after year, writing novels no one would ever read. For decades after her death they languished in a cousin's basement. I took all the handwritten manuscripts that had been kept in shirt boxes and organized them into notebooks. I presented them to my mom after I had read all eight novels and some short stories. I wished I could have told my grandma I understood why she had to write them and why she dreamed of being published.

I am musical and artistic like my mother. She saw beauty

everywhere and taught me more about art than any teacher. As sopranos, we sat in the church choir loft next to each other for decades. We went to art fairs and the Cleveland Museum of Art frequently. Then, I started going to her art openings—a church art show she organized, a one-woman show at the local library. She painted in oils, watercolors, and most expertly in pastels. Her subjects were unusual. She didn't compromise her visions to make money. She seemed to see things others didn't, not just flowers or landscapes.

> My mother wrote:[1]
> "My artwork is composed of places I have been and settings that inspire me. I attempt to work from my own experiences and place myself directly into the painting. I feel that I am basically a value painter because of the wide range of hues from darks to lights which help me convey drama and hold the viewer's interest."

Over the years, my mother didn't sell a lot of work, and she didn't really try, though she was accepted into many juried shows and won awards. She took classes at the community college for so many years that the instructors told her they had nothing left to teach her.

My mother found true freedom when she began to collect a social security check as she had her own money for the first time. She allowed herself to buy more elaborate frames for her paintings and better art supplies. She flourished after the age of 60.

> My mother wrote:
> "Painting, to me, is a way of life. Having been raised in a home where every wall was covered with tasteful artwork created by my brother is something you cannot help but absorb."

Mom spent her last six days in her living room on a hospital bed. The walls were filled with the beauty she created. She had suffered

---

[1] My mother's quotes are from notes she wrote when submitting to the many art shows she entered.

a massive stroke and we brought her home to the untethered and dignified care of hospice. She would look out her front window just as she had when she was a newlywed over 60 years ago, but we do not know if she understood where she was because the stroke had left the artist inside unable to express herself.

*****

Now, I am dismantling the home I grew up in, the house my father and grandfather built, the only safe and immutable refuge of my life. I spend weeks separating my parents' earthly goods into piles for donation or trash. It is agonizing, but the last and worst part is emptying my mother's studio. It holds her life's work, a remarkable journey of skills and beauty, that certainly should be comforting as it is a tangible part of my mother. I feel like a traitor taking it all apart, as if I am undoing everything she accomplished in that space. I want it to stay just as she left it, with every note, sketch, and knickknack in their disordered place. There are scores of pastel portraits of people who modeled for her weekly Friday morning group. I only recognize three people. I will try to find them.

I open a wooden box to see blue and red ribbons: First Place, Second Place, Best in Show, Honorable Mention. There are notes on scrap paper with curious names of paintings: *Bug Off*, *Desert Pollution*, *Harp of Love*, *Hold That Giraffe*, *Chairs of Note*, and a modest notebook listing paintings sold, with the pitiful amount of money paid for decades of skill. The shelves are filled with the odd knickknacks used in still life paintings and binders full of class notes and ideas. A rusty metal cabinet holds boxes of photographs of objects, places, and buildings, from unique angles, meant to inspire new art.

A beautiful portrait of my daughter has hung in the living room for years. One day, while my daughter is helping me clean out the studio, I pull out a framed painting from a crowded corner and it is another portrait of her—one we had never seen. Another day, I find a watercolor of her as a baby. Unexpected gifts left without fanfare.

I donate a beautifully rendered painting of Jesus praying in the desert to the church choir we both belonged to. Often, I sit at rehearsal and look at it. One evening as I'm gazing at it, I see something I never noticed before. Behind a kneeling Jesus, there is a large rock. The rock is cracked in the form of a cross with the shadow of His body hanging from it. It is subtle, but I am still shocked that I have never seen it. Another unexpected gift and a reminder of where my mother is now.

> My mother wrote:
> "While various artists and teachers have influenced me, I would say that the experience of living through the grace of God and hard work have been my best teachers."

*****

There is a last time for everything. After decades of peaceful afternoons, there was a last visit to the Cleveland Museum of Art for us. There was a last time my mother climbed the steps to her studio, and a last time she put down a piece of chalk or a paintbrush. We celebrate the firsts in life—sometimes record them—but we often don't know when the last of something is happening. My mother left a finished watercolor on her studio table with a mat and glass but no frame. I feel an urgency to frame it, to finish the job for her. There is also a very large, unfinished canvas of a vineyard with a scorching sunset in the distance. Two chairs, a table with a wine bottle, and two glasses are in the forefront. The paint is sketchy and the colors simply blocked in, as most painters do to start a scene. But I can imagine her vision, so one day I set up my easel and finish the painting—one last thing we did together.

> Mom, why is this sitting up here in your studio where no one can see it? Can I have it?
>
> Just put "on loan from the artist" on the back so there's no problem, okay? When I'm gone just make a big bonfire and

burn them all! No one will want them anyway!

Mom, are you kidding? We'll be fighting over them.

My brother, sister, and I have had strained relationships during our parents' last years with misperceptions of what we each have done or haven't done. The only thing we fully agree on is that we love our childhood home and are tormented as we empty and prepare to sell it. When the house is finally empty, only the artwork remains.

The three of us gather, and with great effort to be agreeable, we begin the last and most painful task. I am the oldest so I choose first. I select a painting of a young woman sitting with her back to the viewer and facing a stunning orange sunset. My brother chooses, and then my sister. We are solemn and quiet as we assemble our separate piles. My brother likes the more traditional still life subjects, my sister likes the outdoor southwest subjects, and I prefer all the paintings with people in them, so this goes smoothly. Even if there is some disappointment about not getting a certain painting, we keep it to ourselves. Maybe one last gift we can give our mom.

I end up with all the works no one else wants—some curious subjects, some experimental and unfinished pieces. I offer them to my children and cousins, and they take many of them, but an overwhelming amount remains. There are a lot of naked people. Mom used an abundance of colors in the representation of human skin to give it depth and life. These full-length nudes are beautiful but no one chooses to hang them on their walls. I move one of her large, wooden shelving units to my basement to hold the paintings that I am in custody of, but I want them to be seen and enjoyed, not stuck in a furnace room forever.

When Mom was at my house toward the end of her life, I invited friends over for lunch to try to engage her in something besides the television. My neighbors were often called upon to help me get her up or down the three stairs into my house, to pick her up off the floor, to notarize a legal document. I invite each of these kind people to choose a painting. Now, when I visit their homes, I see my mom's artwork displayed and appreciated.

I don't think it was easy for my mother to pursue her gifts, to have the audacity to require a room of her own in a modest bungalow with five people living there. In her generation, there were no expectations of a stay-at-home mom except that she kept her house and children clean. What she accomplished was feminism at its best, in a time when women did not typically ask for what they wanted or have husbands open-minded enough to understand.

> "A woman must have money and a room of her own if she is to write fiction." From Virginia Woolf's *A Room of One's Own*

When I was remarried and in a blended home, I had no little nook of my own. I went from being entirely in charge of a large house to sharing a smaller house with new people, one of them (my stepson) with special physical needs. It took years for me to speak up for myself. I was not a writer by vocation but a school teacher. What right did I have to say, "Family, I am rebranding myself as a writer, and this is what I am in desperate need of now"? When my daughter left home, I claimed her room as my writing space. I share it with a guest bed, toys, and a crib among other things, but it reminds me of my mom's room of her own, and the place where it was possible for her to become an artist.

I tell my daughter that women need to keep reinventing themselves. Latent passions do not need to stay hidden forever, maybe for a season, but not forever. My daughter and I have my mother's example to show us it is possible to go after your passions. Seeing my mother continue to be a prolific artist well into her 80s has shown me that what I create can be an inspiration to my daughter and my granddaughters, now and in the future.

*Take time to write your personal feelings about this singular time in our lives. It may be of great value to future writing.*

Lahore, Pakistan

## *The Mehndi on My Feet*
### Kashaf Ghumman

My back is starting to hurt as I sit still
Waiting for the mehndi on my feet to dry
The cackling hustle of celebration has subsided
As everyone takes their congratulations and their gajras home
I can hear my mother shuffling in the kitchen
She stops
I imagine she's looking around
Taking in the silence
I hear a sniffle
And then she starts shuffling again
She hates dragging her feet but today she allows herself this sin
Her weight is hesitant and uneven in its distribution
Putting too much exertion where her tendons are thinnest
As she slowly settles into the sofa
I can almost hear the creaks in her back and knees
Her joints shifting in a sweet sorrow
The gentle taps on her chest to coax quietness inside her
Tomorrow I will be gone
But our silences will stay here
And from miles away I'll hear her
Aching muscles call me

I get up and walk on the white tiles
No one scolds me or tries to stop me
The mehndi will wash away from the tiles
But I cannot let her be alone in her loneliness

Today we'll rest our stiff backs together
And she can trace her resigned happy-sadness
On the brown-orange streaks on my feet
Tomorrow I'll be gone
But today I am here amah

*Listen to what your body and mind need right now.*

Los Angeles, California

## *displaced*
### Hannah Rousselot

while we were packing
while we were waiting
while I held my suitcase in the smelly airport
while I tried to sleep in a smelly plane

while I clutched my mom's hand and thought
that English sounded like clipped grass

while we drove in this new place
and I counted all the wrong-colored road signs

while we walked through the new door
in the new house in the new town
in the new country in the new language

I thought of my old Little Pony, hair purple
and silken, her skin blue and soft and unyielding.

when we unpacked our bags, she
was nowhere to be found. when we
searched the boxes, she was nowhere
to be found. when we overturned the new place,
she was nowhere to be found.

my parents promised to buy me another,
but with everything going on they forgot.

I didn't mind; anything else would have been a copy.

*Give yourself space to feel your emotions.*

St. Paul, Minnesota

## *Hiraeth*
### Tara Flaherty Guy

My cell phone lit up on my nightstand at 4:16 a.m. with a text message. Although it lacked the alarums-and-excursions terror of an actual phone ringing at that hour, I was still startled by the flare of foot-candle in my dark bedroom. Awakened at midnight by the thunderous **CRACK** of an anonymous aging timber in the house, I'd been lying sleepless ever since. It was January in Minnesota and such explosive, house-shuddering booms weren't exactly uncommon, but this night was extreme. The temperature had plummeted to 30 degrees below zero, and the skeleton of my old house was protesting. I fumbled my phone from the nightstand, curious to identify my co-insomniac and saw a single word glowing in the green text bubble.

### HIRAETH

The word had no meaning to me. Mystified, I squinted and saw that the sender was my 14-year-old niece, Caitlin. The only daughter of my brother, Joey. Another text bubble lit up the room with a question: "Do you know this word?" As the putative wordsmith among my friends and family, such questions were not unusual, not even in the middle of the night when drunken friends now and then texted trivia questions from the bar. But this was Caitlin, who should have been sleeping as if dead in the last hour before her alarm shrilled her awake for school.
I texted back, "Never heard of it . . . definition, please!" Seconds later she sent a hyperlink. I tapped it and the loading circle begin to spin.
A beautiful girl on the knife-edge between girlhood and womanhood, Caitlin was living in her current home with her dad and his current wife. The word "current" had become essential when talking about my brother. With Joey, a recovering alcoholic

and drug addict, all plans were "soft," and all relationships were "fluid." Now and then, this included newly "recovered" addicts he brought home from rehab to stay with him until they could "get on their feet." They often helped themselves to his cash and belongings and terrified Caitlin with unwanted attention before they inevitably decamped for parts unknown. Joey's latest wife—his fourth—was a bipolar nurse named Donna; she didn't much care for Caitlin, and resented Joey's affection for her. If my brother had such a thing, Caitlin was his North Star, the one true light in his life he could navigate by. Despite his flawed parenting, he loved her deeply.

Caitlin's mother, Brandi, was scarcely more stable. She lived in a rented mobile home not far from me in St. Paul, with the latest in a long string of boyfriends. Joey had removed the 14-year-old Caitlin from Brandi's care without protest one recent morning after her boyfriend at the time had fallen asleep on the couch and his bomber joint had lit the living room rug on fire. My niece had unfortunately grown up in chaotic homes, with irresponsible adults, in a dizzying carousel of different towns, her entire life.

It was when, as a little girl, Caitlin experienced her first—but not her last—Christmas with her dad away in a 28-day treatment stay, that she came to cling to me emotionally and physically, with sobs that rent my heart. I knew that in her fractured life I was her rock to cling to, so I held her and rocked her, even as she grew into her teenaged years, and assured her I would always be there for her. Since the age of nine, she had lived with me off and on, as often as I could arrange it. Toward that end, I'd gotten far enough with her parents to secure a signed, but unexecuted, emergency guardianship document. I kept it in my glove box, to show any authority that might need to see it, any time I needed to act on it. I was ready to save her whenever she needed it. Needed me.

The loading circle was still twirling on my phone—the damn cold was even affecting the Internet. As I waited for the web page to finally load, my thoughts turned again to Caitlin's most recent uprooting. Joey and Donna moved 40 miles north of me, to an old house in the woods. She'd made a few friends at her new school, but the area was rural. That meant long school bus rides and kids scattered across miles of countryside. Caitlin had confided that she slept in a partially finished attic, where her wallpaper was ratty old foil covering exposed batts of fiberglass insulation tucked in between the wall studs and her ceiling consisted of sagging cardboard tiles liberally decorated with splotchy, Rorschach-like water stains. She had tried to liven the cheerless surroundings by tacking up her own sketches and artwork on the wall studs, along with a few vintage movie posters, but it remained a windowless, dismal space for a teenager. By my count, this attic room in the old house in the isolated woods constituted Caitlin's 11th "home" in 14 years.

The website finally loaded, with a direct link to a definition:

>   **HIRAETH** – NOUN (Welsh)
>   An intense longing or grief felt for a home to which you cannot return, or which may never have been

Then, a new text from her lit up my phone, displaying a single sentence:

> "It's how I've always felt."

An image of Caitlin, awake in the darkness of her unfinished attic room, grieving for a home she never had, never felt, flashed into my mind. I leapt out of bed. I was up and moving, pulling on jeans and a parka over my nightgown, thrusting my feet into cold boots, running out the door into the frigid predawn. A minute later, I was in my car and on the road, driving north to Caitlin, under the glittering, indifferent stars, to bring my niece home.

> "... may there come across the waters a path of yellow moonlight to bring you safely home." ~John O'Donohue

## *A Recipe for Greek Bread*
### Catherine A. Coundjeris

It's sweet and surprising—
the staff of life.
Baked to remember Nana;
baked to remember Dad
gone 10 years ago on October 12th.

Made from scratch a last will and testament.
Set aside yeast in a bowl of warm water.
Tsoureki bread–Sunday bread.
Mix with Anatolian spices:
one teaspoon of mahaleb
and four grains of mastic that
my oldest sister buys in Cleveland.

Grind together with
cinnamon, anise seeds, and
orange peel in a handheld pestle for old times' sake.
Boil in a pot with one bay leaf.
Heat milk, add butter.

A recipe shaped by my grandmother,
nourishment for generations,
I press and form
pleased by the dough's texture.
Its aroma filling the kitchen,
surrounding me in warm memories.

Mix unsifted flour, sugar, and salt.
Shape a hole and pour in the yeast,
milk and butter, spices, add three eggs.
Fold it gently towards the middle.

Work by kneading until dough is smooth
and feels right—smooth and firm.
Let rise for six hours.
Perfect fare for Easter.

Punch down and paint with egg yolk.
Sprinkle with sesame seeds.
Sometimes I braid a cross upon it;
other times I let it go unadorned.
Simply bread enough to feed our family
for days and days.

Bread that smells like Nana's house.
Bread, butter, and good strong coffee
create a tangible link to the old ways
for my half-Greek bones.
Faith and family mingling in my mind
like food color on hard-boiled eggs
nesting on top of the fancy loaf.

*Live each day to the fullest. You can dream and accomplish
even while sheltering in place. Remember this shall pass.*

**South Hadley, Massachusetts**

## *Blackamora\**
J.L. Lapinel

The hum of a tractor
breathes soft, in the distance,
the faint change of gears
and the neigh of a mare.
The stallion gives answer
alone in his paddock
and the crickets of evening
prepare for their sing.

Brother is mowing,
Mother cooks dinner,
and Father wipes sweat
off his brow
with an arm.
A woman's shrill call
lingers faint, in the distance,
then falls off to silence
unanswered, again.

Soft children's laughter
floats off down the mountain,
and the hay blows in waves
through the field where I lie.
Mother can't find me
to know I can hear her
as the sun's rays are fading
and the mares chew their hay.

*Blackamora was my family's small farm in upstate New York. The name was inspired by the song "How are things in Glocca Morra" from the film *Finian's Rainbow*.

*It's important to allow ourselves permission to climb inside
and tend to our quiet voices.*

Chicago, Illinois

## *After Georgia O'Keeffe's* Spring *1923/24*
### Cynthia Gallaher

The weather vane pointed west,
but we never left Chicago
that spring after father died.

My mother hand-scraped, whitewashed
garage and clothesline posts herself.
There was never such splendor as

lilac bushes in our alley.
I remember autumns more,
burning bushelsful of leaves and

Mother raking ashes.

*If you have one, enjoy your backyard, your deck, or back porch. Maybe grow a garden or a pot of herbs.*

## *Blooms*
### Andrée Rose Catalfamo

I'm at my mom's house, a rancher in a newish development near Rehoboth Beach, Delaware. I'm where every good daughter should be on Mother's Day, unless she's a mother herself, that is. Mom and I sit at her dining room table, sipping coffee, while my brother Dominic, who is also visiting, lounges on the living room sofa, listening to some sports show on headphones.

My brother is two-and-a-half years younger than me. He was born a week after my father's father died, in June of 1964. The Italian tradition is to name the grandson after the grandfather, and so Dominic is named, which makes me wonder about the transference of souls and such. No, that can't really be, because Dominic's soul definitely came from someplace other than Highlandtown, Baltimore.

When Dom was born, the umbilical cord was wrapped around his neck, and he lost oxygen to his brain for three seconds. Three seconds to dictate the course of a life: my brother suffered brain damage as a result of the asphyxiation. The damage shows up in odd places.

I ask Mom what she wants to do for her day.

"Let's go to Peppers," she says. Peppers is the nursery down the road from Mom's development. "I want to get some plants for my garden."

I'm happy to oblige as I'd rather pay for something she wants than shell out for a gift card or a trip to an expensive restaurant, neither of which I'm sure she'd like.

Us three pile into her PT Cruiser and head for Peppers. Mom drives, Dom rides shotgun, and I sit in the back. As I get in, I bop his bald head in what we both know is a loving gesture, and we settle in for the trip.

"Hey Ange," he says to me now, as we head down the narrow country road. "Did you know that in 1970, when the Orioles won the Series, we had four 20 game winners? Can you name 'em? I can! Palmer, Cuellar, Dobson, and McNally!"

Dominic knows things. While he can tell you Cal Ripken's batting average in 1985 or the call letters for the CBS affiliate in San Francisco, he can't follow directions that have any more than two steps or add a column of numbers without difficulty. To say he has Rain Man qualities is to stereotype him, but he possesses that baffling combination of facility with long-term memory and a lack of intellectual capability. He lives largely in the now, which is both admirable and frightening beyond measure.

It's crowded at the garden center, as many grateful children of all ages buy flowers and seedlings and trees for their mothers. Mom trots ahead to where the tomato plants are housed under a thick plastic tent. Dominic follows, pushing a shopping cart. I trail behind, touching leaves and admiring blooms.

I'm amused by a young family of five pulling three ficus trees on a flatbed wagon. Two preteen boys control the handle while their little sister rides on the wagon, seated among the trees, laughing as the leaves brush her face. The father looks at me and smiles broadly as I pass them.

So much life in these greenhouses! I feel my spirits lift as I drift through the aisles of flowers, fruits, veggies, and herbs. One room full of herbs especially intrigues me: it's lavish and wild and rampant with scent.

In another time and place, I had an herb garden. I grew all sorts: rosemary, thyme, lavender, chives, oregano, cilantro, sage. I used to love gently pinching their leaves and then sniffing my fingers to take in their delicate scents. It's been a long time, and life events have led me to believe that my green thumb has turned black. However, as I roam through the aisles of this herbal wonderland, I decide that in addition to buying Mom's presents, I'll gift myself a few plants and see if I can still make something grow.

Mom decides on a number of veggie starters, some pansies, and a vivid purple fuchsia. We buy clay pots and a bag of potting soil. I slip a white window box into the cart and choose, for myself, three plants from the riot of herbs, as well as a baby jade. Dom turns the cart over to me and wanders the aisles, a gentle giant in a lush fragrant jungle.

When Dom was a little boy, he was neither calm nor placid. He was a holy terror. I remember him ripping and tearing through the house, a human Rock 'Em Sock 'Em robot. He colored on the walls. He smeared poop on his bed. He knew no boundaries because he couldn't think to have any. I was scared of him even though I'm older and back then could have taken him in a fair fight. Mostly. Our fistfights were epic. See, due to being walloped on a regular basis, I developed a jamming uppercut and figured out a way to wrestle him into a half nelson and then drag him across the floor like George of the Jungle. That all stopped the day that he punched me harder than Rocky socked Apollo Creed and I saw stars. I knew then that he was stronger than me and I put an end to the fist fighting once and for all.

Schooling the pugnacious, rebellious Dom was a challenge for my mother. First, she had to fight my father's misguided idea that Dominic could be "normal." When Dad first heard my mother use the word "retarded," for that was the term back then, he got so incensed that he threw his dinner plate against the wall and then beat my mother for a half hour until she cowered in the corner and pleaded for mercy while I screamed and my brother threw his peas and carrots all over the floor. My father couldn't stand the thought that his boy wasn't going to make the grade. He demanded that Dominic go to "regular school."

Mom tried to comply, enrolling Dominic in the elementary school up the street from us. However, "mainstreaming," as it is now required by the public schools, didn't exist in those days. So, Dominic, with his special brew of cognitive and behavioral issues, was a kindergarten washout because of his wild behavior, which teachers didn't know how to deal with back then.

Despite my father's protests, the school system sent Dominic to The Chimes, a school for the "mentally retarded." But that wasn't right either and everyone soon knew it, especially when Dom cut out and assembled an eerily accurate cardboard replica of the school bus that would come to pick him up each day.

"Look, Mom! Open, close! Open, close!"

He'd assembled the bus complete with a door and lever that would swing open and shut. Dom had something going for him, it had to be said. He advanced to the St. Francis School for Special Education, where he learned to read and write alongside kids with Down's syndrome, behavioral issues, and other brain trauma. The nuns were kind and stern by turns and wielded the pointer to painful effect. Eventually, they managed to turn the wild child into a calm, caring boy and taught him to read, write, and do a little math. Later, Dom would go to St. Elizabeth's School for Habilitation, a special high school where he'd learn workplace skills as well as academics.

I catch up with Dom at Peppers and see that he's talking with a guy who's wearing an Orioles shirt.

"Yeah, they shoulda won that one last night," I hear the guy say.

"You said it, man. But our bullpen stinks. And we need a whole new front office, don't ya think? Fire Angelos!"

The new buddies slap five and continue to yap on about the merits of the home team.

Dom isn't afraid of talking to anyone; he has no shyness whatsoever. I've been to more than one sporting event with him during which he manages to befriend every single person in the rows in front of and in back of us. Sometimes his gregariousness puts people off, because they don't know how to treat someone who operates with a total lack of guile. But Dom is charming and they usually stay long enough to let him win them over. Dom has season tickets to the Orioles, and the people who sit near him call him Cheese because he's always smiling.

Now Dom laughs in his cheesy way as he says goodbye to his

new friend.

    Mom's ready to go, so we cash out and run to the car with our plants and pots through a gusty, drenching spring shower. I catch a chill.

    Back at Mom's house, I have a hot bath to warm up. I love the giant tub in her master bathroom. The only thing I don't like is that it's surrounded on three sides by floor-to-ceiling mirrors. I sit naked at the tub's edge, confronted times three by my plump, middle-aged, nonchild-bearing body. I survey the years as they show themselves on my skin. I know I'm lovable, but I don't love the moon-surface thighs and Michelin-tire-man roll around my middle. I play hide-and-seek with my reflection until the water is just the right temperature and then I slide in. The water always comforts me when I start thinking about what might have been.

    Around 5 p.m., it's stopped raining and a late afternoon sun emerges.

    "Do you want to pot the plants?" Mom asks me.

    I hesitate, because I just got out of the bathtub. But Mom can be quite persuasive, and anyway, I really should transfer my little fledglings into their homes.

    "Sounds like a great idea," I reply, hoping that my lack of enthusiasm doesn't show.

    We drag the seedlings, pots, and potting soil around to the back of the house, arrange everything on the deck table, and proceed to get our hands dirty. I observe and try to mimic the depth of the holes she digs, how she situates each plant, the distance between them. You'd think that I would know how to do this by now, but there's always a relearning in every growing season. And while I think of myself as a nurturing soul, I also know that I've never had to do it enough for it to embed in my muscle memory, the way that mothers do, the way that they are, the way they need to be.

    Into a deep green pot goes my baby jade while the cilantro, basil, and rosemary are nestled into the window box. We make a hanging basket burst with purple and yellow pansies. I can tell that my mother is content with these simple gestures; she smiles softly and whispers sotto voce as she tucks each plant into its new home.

Then Mom asks Dominic to go with her out to her garden. I watch from afar as together they plant the tomatoes, zucchini, and eggplant starters. Mom tells Dom where to dig the holes, and he dutifully obeys.

As I look at the both of them, I think, *He is good, my brother. He is mine: my dowry, my conscience, my inspiration.* I see his soft brown eyes in my dreams sometimes and wake with a heartache. *How will the rest of his life go, especially after our mother is no longer here to guide him? Will I be enough? Will I be able to show him how to plant?*

*"I don't think of the misery, but of all the beauty that still remains."* ~Anne Frank

## *Uninvited*
### Robinwyn Lewis

The wild invades
my garden. Spring beauties puncture
careful borders, onions
pierce their green spears through
the sedum, dandelions swirl
brown-tipped floss among the iris,
compact mounds of unnamed yellow flowers
rise in random places.

Weeds, my neighbor calls them.
Spray before they take control.

Too late.

And anyway,

there is something
does not love
too tame a garden,
pushes these invaders
through hard ground.
They add the unexpected to the measured.

Live and let live, I tell my neighbor,
(curiosity and laziness my guides).
Her garden boasts strict order, brilliant flowers,
but in my garden wonders still surprise.

*One day at a time.*

Nanaimo, British Columbia, Canada

## *Movement in the Cinnabar Valley*
Nichola Ruddell

Winter's veil has lifted
light touches everything
in this hour of possibility
everything is awakened
Birds seize the open sky
The Bleeding Hearts
splashed across our hills
dangle their delicate jewels
in perfect rows
The Dogwood
in her
fleeting beauty
a beacon for a moment
quickly unfolds
While
deep in the forest
draped in emerald blankets
the mighty Cedar
sway in the wind
and in all this beauty

We hold on

*I am healthy and strong in spirit, mind, and body.*

Bloomfield, New Jersey

## *On the Cover: Couch*
### Ann Marie Sekeres

Digital drawing of me drawing on the iPad, two silly cats, and a glass of wine.

I drew this in January 2020 on just a normal winter day, when you stay inside because it's too cold and raw and unpleasant outside. I didn't dream of what it would mean now.

I'm very inspired by the younger illustrators I see, but despite my efforts I don't think my drawings look quite like theirs. I believe there is just a natural generational difference. Since I learned digital drawing so much later than my original art education, I find I build my works like real-world techniques. This work is structured like a cut paper collage.

*We're not just working at home. We're trying to get work done during a devastating global crisis.*

# *Contributors*

**Paula Bonnell's** poems have appeared in *APR*, *The Hudson Review*, *Rattle*, and dozens more, nationally and internationally, and won awards from *Kalliope*, *Negative Capability*, New England Poetry Club, Chester H. Jones Foundation, and the City of Boston. Her 2017 chapbook *tales retold* follows three collections: *Airs & Voices*, selected by Mark Jarman for a Ciardi Prize; *Before the Alphabet*, a kindergarten story; and *Message*, a debut, including "Midwest," as heard on *The Writer's Almanac*, and "Eurydice," chosen by Albert Goldbarth for a *Poet Lore* publication award. Paula, a PEN New England Discovery writer, has also published fiction, essays, and book reviews.

**Andrée Rose Catalfamo** is a writer and instructor working in creative nonfiction, fiction, and poetry. Although she holds both an MA and a PhD in Education, last year she returned to Wilkes University to begin an MA in Creative Writing. Somehow, she is managing to teach rhetoric and composition at SUNY Cortland while pursuing her studies and working on a memoir. A Baltimore, Maryland native, Andrée misses Fells Point, crab cakes, and the American Visionary Art Museum, as well as her family and friends. Andrée lives happily with her partner, the poet Burt Myers, in Binghamton, New York.

**Lindsey Clark** is a Wisconsin native who has lived in Massachusetts, North Carolina, California, Colorado, Italy, Morocco, Madagascar, and Antarctica—along the way exploring more than 60 countries on every continent. Her work has been published in magazines such as *Hippocampus*, *daCunha*, *Switchback*, *Newfound*, and *South 85*, as well as the anthology "Memories of Sun." She has a piece forthcoming in the *Shanghai Literary Review* and is also the author of a travel memoir, "Land of Dark and Sun."

**Catherine A. Coundjeris**, a former elementary school teacher, has also taught writing at Emerson College and ESL writing at Urban College in Boston, Massachusetts. Her work is published in literary magazines, including *34th Parallel Magazine, Borrowed Solace, Ariel Chart, New Readers Magazine, The Drabble, Backchannels,* and *Inkling Magazine* of *The Storyteller's Cottage*. Currently she is living with her family in Frederick, Maryland and working on a YA novel. Catherine volunteers as an ESL Coordinator with the Literacy Council of Frederick County and she is very passionate about adult literacy.

**Diane Vogel Ferri** is a teacher, poet, and writer living in Solon, Ohio. Her essays have been published in *Scene Magazine, Cleveland Stories, Cleveland Christmas Memories, Raven's Perch, Good Works Review,* and by Cleveland State University, among others. Her poems can be found in numerous journals such as *Plainsongs, Rubbertop Review,* and *Poet Lore*. She has a chapbook, *Liquid Rubies,* and a book, *The Volume of Our Incongruity,* published. She has done many poetry readings locally. Her novel, *The Desire Path,* can be found on Amazon. Diane's essay, "I Will Sing for You," was featured at the Cleveland Humanities Festival in 2018. A former teacher, she holds an MEd from Cleveland State University. She has an Author Page on Facebook for current news and is a founding member of Literary Cleveland.

**Cynthia Gallaher**, a Chicago-based poet, is author of four poetry collections, including *Epicurean Ecstasy: More Poems About Food, Drink, Herbs and Spices,* and three chapbooks, including *Drenched*. The Chicago Public Library lists her among its "Top 10 Requested Chicago Poets."

**Kashaf Ghumman** is a doctor from Pakistan, trying to learn the rhythms of the medical field while studying the anatomy of poetry. She has previously been published in the *Shot Glass Journal* by Muse Pie Press, Recenter Press, *Glintmoon, Revolute Magazine, Backchannels Journal,* and *Breadcrumbs Magazine*.

**Tara Flaherty Guy** is a recovering zoning enforcement officer with a BA in Creative Writing from Metropolitan State University in St. Paul, Minnesota. She is a contributing writer at St. Paul Publishing Company. Her work is forthcoming in the *St. Paul Almanac, Minnesota Voices Poetry Journal*, and *Talking Stick/Jackpine Writers' Bloc*. She lives in Minnesota with her husband and three cheeky, entitled cats.

**Jo Ann Hoffman** is a writer, editor, and former communications director whose publications include a children's book, short fiction, and poems in literary journals, including *The Merton Quarterly, Pinesong, Kakalak, Flying South, Red Clay Review, Snapdragon,* and *New Verse News*, among others. She has received contest awards from the Palm Beach Poetry Festival, Carteret Writers, and Pamlico Writers. Her nonfiction book, *Angels Wear Black*, recounts the only technology executive kidnapping to occur in California's Silicon Valley. A native of Toledo, Ohio, she and her husband now live in Cary and Beaufort, North Carolina.

**Ann Howells** edited *Illya's Honey* for 18 years. Her books include *Under a Lone Star, Cattlemen & Cadillacs*, an anthology of D/FW poets she edited, *So Long As We Speak Their Names*, and *Painting the Pinwheel Sky*. Her four chapbooks include *Black Crow in Flight*, published through Main Street Rag's 2007 competition, and *Softly Beating Wings*, which won the 2017 William D. Barney competition. Ann's work appears in *Spillway, Little Patuxent Review,* and *The Langdon Review*, among others. She has been nominated seven times for a Pushcart Prize.

**Stephanie Kadel Taras** has authored multiple books in 20 years as a freelance writer in Ann Arbor, Michigan, including the award-winning college history *On Solid Rock* and memoir *Mountain Girls*. Her work has also been published in *Bear River Review, Belle Journal,* and *Ann Arbor Observer*.

**Roberta S. Kuriloff**, is an author, speaker, attorney, and community activist. She has published *Everything Special, Living Joy*, prose and poems to inspire. She is presently writing narrative nonfiction about building the home of her dreams in the Maine woods, reflecting on her life journey of spiritual and personal exploration that gave her a new definition of home as a place where heart, love, and joy thrive. She previously was a founding member of two domestic violence projects and an elderly services organization, as well as a Hospice volunteer and bereavement workshop facilitator. Her passions are writing and dance.

**J.L. Lapinel** is a poet and educator from Manhattan living in New England. Her work appears in *The Wellington Street Review, Quill Books, Front Runner Quarterly, Wide Open Magazine, The Cambridge Collection, The North American Poetry Review, Odessa Poetry Review, Minetta Review*, and *The Tin Penny*. She was nominated for a Pushcart Prize in 2019. She holds a BA in Literature and Creative Writing and an MA in Literature, both from New York University. She is presently an MFA candidate at UMass Amherst.

**Robinwyn Lewis** grew up near Chicago, Illinois. She got her BA in Russian at Swarthmore College, an MA in Russian at UPenn, and a law degree from George Washington University. In 1981, she went to work for the United States Navy as a civilian attorney from which she retired in 2007. This has allowed her to indulge her long-term interests in writing, painting, and music, and time to enjoy her family. She has been teaching English as a second language for 10 years and is currently working on an MA in TESOL at UMBC. You can see her artwork at robinwyn.com.

**Carolyn Martin**, from associate professor of English to management trainer and currently retiree, has journeyed from New Jersey through California to Oregon to discover Douglas firs, months of rain, and dry summers. Her poems and book reviews have appeared in publications throughout North America, Australia, and the United Kingdom, and her fourth collection, *A Penchant for Masquerades*, was released in 2019. She is currently the poetry editor of *Kosmos Quarterly: journal for global transformation*. Find out more about Carolyn at carolynmartinpoet.com.

**Crystal Leigh Melbourne** is a starry-eyed poet based in Europe, who often writes about her dreams of a better world and a fervent passion for the ocean. She's endlessly enthusiastic about well-resolved emotional intelligence and is currently working on her first poetry chapbook on the subject. You can keep up with her on Instagram @cmelbourne.poetry.

**Courtney Essary Messenbaugh** is a practiced dilettante and has been everything from a waitress to a political fundraiser to a bond analyst. She has climbed a big mountain in Tanzania, lived in Switzerland, New York, and Chicago, Illinois, and loves to laugh and try new things. She currently lives in Colorado and delights in the blanket of neon blue sky there. Courtney is mother to three wildling children, wife to one husband, and best friend to one Muppet-looking dog. She is relatively new to the poetry world and is thrilled to be a part of **HOME**.

**Sara Palmer** wrote her first poem in second grade. Since then, poetry has been her vehicle for self-expression, healing, and enjoyment. During her career as a psychologist, Sara specialized in emotional and social aspects of disability, chronic illness, and caregiving. She published articles and chapters for professionals and several books for patients and families, most recently *Living with HHT: Understanding and Managing Your Hereditary Hemorrhagic Telangiectasia*. Now retired from psychology, she devotes more time to creative writing and volunteer work. Sara is on the Boards of Cure HHT and Yellow Arrow Publishing. She lives in Baltimore, Maryland with her husband and dog and enjoys close ties with her adult children, two young grandchildren, and numerous friends.

**Kara Panowitz** thrives on creating through writing, theatre, photography, and filmmaking, among other arts. She received both her BA in Theatre and her MA in Social Work from the University of Maryland. Kara works for an anti-hunger nonprofit and is the acting Executive Director of Megaphone Project. Previously, she has been a Peace Corps Volunteer in Madagascar, a Special Ed and ESL teacher in Baltimore, Maryland, and a bartender in Australia.

**Hannah Rousselot** (she/her) is a queer French-American poet, writer, and educator. Her work revolves around her experiences with mental illness, love, loss, and her connection to the world. Her poetry has appeared in many publications, including *Parentheses Magazine*, *The McNeese Review*, *The Blue Nib*, and *The Broadkill Review*, among others. Her first collection of poetry, *Fragments of You*, is available for purchase. You can follow her work at Facebook.com/hmrpoetry or Twitter @hannahrousselot.

**Nichola Ruddell** was born in Vancouver, British Columbia and raised on Salt Spring Island. She attended university at the University of Victoria, receiving a degree in Child and Youth Care. She is also a Phoenix Rising Yoga Therapist. She enjoys writing poetry and is previously published in the online magazine *Literary Mama*. After living in many places with her family she has made a home in Nanaimo, British Columbia with her husband and two young children.

**Ann Marie Sekeres** went to art school and learned to paint a long time ago. She showed a bit around New York in the 1990s but didn't get where she wanted to be. She became a very happy museum and nonprofit publicity director and started a family. She found out about the Procreate drawing app from an illustrator she hired, stole her kid's iPad, and has been drawing every day since. Follow her work on Instagram @annmarieprojects.

**Sarah Smith** is a Baltimore, Maryland librarian. She loves pinball, sheet cake, and anything athletic. Her work has been featured in *the light ekphrastic*, "Smile, Hon, You're in Baltimore," and *City Paper*. She blogs at hampdenunicorn.com.

**Amy Soricelli** has been published in numerous publications and anthologies, including *Dead Snakes, Corvus Review, Deadbeats, Long Island Quarterly, Voice of Eve, The Muddy River Poetry Review, Pangolin Review, Plum Tree Tavern, Red Queen Literary Magazine, Terse Journal, Ethel5, Stirring: A Literary Collection, Thirty West, Remington Review, Allegro Poetry, 8 Poems, THAT Literary Review, The Westchester Review, Nixes Mate Review, Sparks of Calliope*, and many others. She published a chapbook, *Sail Me Away*, in 2019. She was nominated by Billy Collins for an Emerging Writer's Fellowship 2019 and for Sundress Publications "Best of the Net" 2013, and was a recipient of the Grace C. Croff Poetry Award, Lehman College, 1975.

**Elizabeth Spencer Spragins** is a poet and writer who taught in North Carolina community colleges for more than a decade. Her tanka and bardic verse in the Celtic style have been published extensively in Europe, Asia, and North America. She is the author of *With No Bridle for the Breeze: Ungrounded Verse* and *The Language of Bones: American Journeys Through Bardic Verse*. Updates are available on her website: www.authorsden.com/elizabethspragins. An avid swimmer and an enthusiastic fiber artist, she lives in Fredericksburg, Virginia.

**Yvonne**, first poetry editor of two pioneer feminist magazines, *Aphra* and *Ms.*, has received several awards, including from the National Endowment for the Arts for poetry (1974, 1984) and the Leeway Foundation for fiction (2003, as Yvonne Chism-Peace). Recent print publications include *Is It Hot In Here Or Is It Just Me?* (Beautiful Cadaver Project: Social Justice Anthologies), *Home: An Anthology*, *Quiet Diamonds* (2018, 2019), *161 One-Minute Monologues from Literature*, *Philadelphia Stories*, *Metonym*, *Colere*, *Dappled Things*, *Burningword Literary Journal*, *Bryant Literary Review*, *Pinyon*, *Nassau Review*, *Bosque Press #8*, and *Foreign Literary Journal #1*. She is the author of an epic trilogy: *Iwilla Soil*, *Iwilla Scourge*, and *Iwilla Rise*. Selected online publications can be accessed at iwilla.com.

Made in the USA
Middletown, DE
10 June 2020